MELANIE'S BOOK

MELANIE'S BOOK

Melanie's Book

KELVIN CORCORAN

Simple Vice
&
West House Books

First published in 1996
by Simple Vice
& West House Books
West House
Broad Street
Hay-on-Wye
via Hereford HR3 5DB

Printed in England by
Joshua Horgan Print Partnership

A CIP record for this book is available
from the British Library

ISBN 0 9521891 4 3

NOTES AND ACKNOWLEDGEMENTS

Some of these poems have appeared in the following :
Grille; *Eonta*; *Angel Exhaust*; *Oasis*; *Exact Change Yearbook*
(Carcanet) and *Conductors of Chaos* (Picador). Grateful
acknowledgements to them all.

Snow has fallen all night,
whiteness blurs the street
muffling incoming calls,
you can't get out, even if you wanted to.

I woke to tell you something,
dreaming of the baby
half formed under the driven sky,
the blizzard turns about.

All our names made vague
block the roads out of town,
a tangle of limbs, two lives,
caught in the drift of speech.

In the snow all over England
we look for the candid word.

February sun burns low in the sky,
second sight glazed by refraction
punches a hole in the white world,
admitting fields of gleaming snow.

The black road, like a river,
rushes in from both sides, talking
goes on and on to the first moment,
falling backwards into lyric
through a hedge of bright ignorance,
cutting out the shape already lived with;
the dark engraved capital
half buried in that narrow space,
echoes the message landscape
walking with you to the house.

Driving through town, Saturday morning,
this winter's credit squeeze
makes unaccustomed space all round,
how can you lose, so bright and cheery?

Soon all of this will be library pictures,
like the war of library pictures
strikes the coded air, incoming then gone,
each day reconstructed.

You mustn't know any of this:
the roar of prayers and aircraft,
sirens sound in Jerusalem, Jerusalem the golden,
the war zone burning Sumeria.

Use the correct form of expression:
the war is good and bad for business.

Wait for the light under a canopy of leaves,
casual music burning the crisis,
time to get literal, the man said to the man
message comes out all the same.

Estate by estate, family by family
the poor turned invisible,
in the hard blue sky above the stadium
currencies vanish, nations appear.

Saturation coverage tells you nothing
I was thinking in the water, on my knees,
the new year rolling across the park,
you already know it's poetry.

Men walk like this, women walk like that.
Our sense of purpose would stun the traffic.

Portland Plymouth London Irish Sea
severe gale force nine
funneled through the channel,
roaring at the window night.

Who sang the song that went
forget the past, trust to speed,
waiting for the one sign
big sky fairing in the west?

The harbour landscaped out of memory
reappears ranch style,
like a thought that won't shift
battered in and out of dream.

All day its tinny music keeps us warm:
all night we float on darker sound.

Awake out of the window I saw
the dark towers of the women,
a grainy woodcut against the glow of the city
spread out like a fresh map.

The north door opens, only one word,
we find the body difficult to speak;
corridors of sea flooding the streets,
the great stink of it just around the corner.

This is not the voice of an actor,
making the word nation an embarrassment
politicians praising other politicians:
wash of salt staining the lot.

For Madeleine

Fields turn all afternoon
white blossom fills the mind,
sparrows chirp and our faces gape
at the green shoots of the work itself.

One step away from spring
blinking out of the tunnel,
even the traffic knows Eros
breathing cold April all around.

Her name in gentleness surrounds me.
Her hair a white river floods over me.

The family radio was smaller than the fat battery attached to it. We kept it in a tin; twanging Duane Eddy, the Shadows and assassinations echoed out of a metallic past. Its casing was sky blue with a silver plastic grid over the small speaker. The transparent, circular tuner had a serrated edge for a better grip. A blood red line picked out Athens, Moscow, Luxembourg, Athlone.
O city city. Turning. Turning.

*

Over a doorway in the museum hangs the salutation to Parnassus, 1904. At the prow the leader raises a chalice. A dozen red, fleshy men eyeing each others' muscles, row towards the distant mountain. You see this from the bow facing the toiling pairs, caught in Biblical exertion as the choppy waves break on rocks. Truth spills out of the picture, the chain that is round us now.

My arsonist neighbour lights another fire
dirtying the end of summer, Moscow burns,
smoke thickens - ignore the words, listen to the tone.
Can you cope with this one in a golfing suit?

The room fills with smoke and all sense evacuates
- if I stood up straight the line would be unimpeded -
and longer than all the seasons rising above the white desk,
he lost the inward walk, promenading frames at an exhibition.

Variously orchestrated the moon rests on the hill;
the air is softer than a hidden message,
the airwaves carrying Russian music, American poetry.
We'll conspire to forget the world, whatever it says.

There are moments of Biblical rhetoric here
above the loaded tray, telephone, assumed narrative;
I would rather talk to you in the light,
not rub anger into it at 2 o'clock, 3 o'clock.

We float away from England, mapping the brittle voices;
our house at night is full of noise, ringed by fire
- if this is what happens I feel cheated -
and nocturnal animals pull at the rubbish for love.

If I stood up straight the line would be unimpeded.

Earth at night is an uneven smear of lights;
America, Europe, parts of Asia, the Gulf,
fires burning in rural tracts cash the crop.
It's homely, a light left on in the dark;
earth at night is the pattern of money,
a squid fleet off Japan, gas flares at sea.

Below red cliffs in the narrow channel
the days pile up in line astern,
stupid in the mouth of the good time.
The trade route takes you anywhere;
along the streets of a new nation
imagine the film of all these faces.

In our lives country music's literal,
sounding out the low place of compromise
the money sets in all our hands;
we turn into the darker wave,
we touch the ground and keep the deal:
a river of silk pours over the desert.

*

Clematis float outside the window,
watery stars riding the air.
I hope you read this soon, written over, thick with dust,
I hope you see the free state rising,
not just a green place, with good sport
for English power to set its foot.

The bosses have all gone for the season,
one block of light falls across the corridor,
quiet after business don't walk away from love.
Curvey T martins bomb the gardens,
that's all my life in the bowl of summer
- I am out of the way of it at present.

I am drunk thinking about you,
the birds twittering hole the sky,
their sharp black beaks drilling
the other side where everything happens,
like the single song from your red mouth.
What happened to you? (I mean who)

*

There was much fatuous surprise at the endurance of the right;
its invention of the common view and resurgence in the hearts
supposedly sung for.
The shift workers didn't wait for the rconstructed ballads.
Leaning against a wall you just want noise out of your ears,
hands
out of filth, one breath of fresh air.
We're happy stupid inside the garden, wrapped in thin profit,
untouched
and grinning.
- I thought it was my life, my family.

*

11

I run into the cool morning;
rooks study the rubble of the pavilion,
a motorbike buried in the hedge,
the day laid out in swift decline.

Disintegrate the myth of speed
was all she said, a blown code,
the white and staring sky
rises behind the glowing houses.

The recession is over/deepening
the new estate on the edge,
securing its inhabitants
breaking bargains in a ring.

Running under Venus
straight into the ditch,
a white hole burnt in everything I see,
face flat to the cold ground.

In the middle of the journey,
the straight way lost,
we came to a dark wood.

Pine needles for bed,
branches spread across a sky without depth,
you felt the earth swallow you whole.

Your cry startled a bird
Your breathing the beat of wings,
April sun ascending.

We came to a dark wood.

There I'm thinking with my hands
and the room's flying over the city,
over the bridge, the parks and zippy motorway
your open face floating before me.

Everytime I see you
something happens and I can't speak,
like birds in the air
calling and calling your name out.

That will do in plain speech
against what we don't know,
the burning traffic takes us
wrecked on the far side.

There aerial words wait,
unequal to your next breath.

In the dark car staring
the whole sky unfolds before us,
over the fields and silent roads where we must go,
your face and the stars
and the great John James line,
'...here in this your poem and mine. I beg you to free this boy.'

Whilst other activities tap the window
we move inside each other,
your perfectbody calling and calling glides over me
tier upon tier I rise in cathedral light,
my mouth opening inside you,
in all this darkness only your taste,

Here in this your underworld and mine
I beg you to keep this boy.

Night rushes in at the car window
lighted houses and cold miles westward,
later, in the hotel we hear
voices going home drift away
and an owl calling over the border
over the dark hills and rivers,
there your face is changing above me;
love pours into us and we cross the threshold
writing a page from Melanie's book
- nobody has loved me the way you do.

*

Inanna Queen of Heaven and Earth
everything flows from you, you go to hell for your lover.
You're the Queen of Heaven and Earth, I thought you'd want to
know.
- You know how to stop a girl eating her breakfast don't you.

*

Out into the white morning
we were surprised to see other people alive
going about their normal business,
for we know this world is uninhabited.

The river rose in the night
flooding the winter fields,
a slow thought emerges,
frozen by morning.

All this landscape stuff?
Just ice age mud and trees,
I suppose I live here now,
unpeopled more or less.

At night we burn,
I look into your face
and the world's made dark
in the music of your red mouth.

Thy faire vertues move me,
not to use one word for another,
perfect sexual beauty
say my name over and over.

Moonlight pales the dark river
revealing the banks where lives are broken,
the distant hills emerge as negatives
and the sky's gone to another country.

My brother's name is Babylon and
if you kill me he'll kill you.
I am not there, between one town and the next,
the fields laid out for spring.

Look when I take my hand from you
how white it is   shining shining
I once held love in that hand

*

Driving with him at night
she sees the road running parallel
known only by the lights of other cars
and thinks - my life is perfect.

*

I see you float on quilted water
another room somewhere, head back
right thigh resting on the left
as if to take a step

Turning in your sleep
lifted by the dark wave
silver hoops catch the light
I want you   I want you   I want you.

In the middle of the journey,
the straight way lost,
we came to a dark wood.

Pine trees for bed,
branches spread across a sky without depth,
you felt the earth swallow you whole.

Your cry startled a bird
Your breathing the beat of wings,
April sun ascending.

We came to a dark wood.

Restore us song on Sion Hill,
it would be saturday, lodged against the note
- insert after April poem.

As the crow flies over the 14 wires of the street
weather caught messages;
artefact, lime tree, the first place will out.

Then I knew what I couldn't face,
at the dark end of the street
the great awakening.

Restore us song on Sion Hill.

One night we walked across town under the blown stars, with
all the damage at our backs it does not come well arranged.
Dark houses piled up; try lust, pride and covetousness. Try
closing the door on that lot, domestic gardens alive with those
animals.

We saw the fox eyeing cars, staring into the moment of impact
then sauntering off the road, to leave a fox-shaped hole in the
air, for all the traffic in the world to drive through.

Dark houses piled up. Close the door. The fox stepping in and
out of life in
front of us.

One morning the sound of horses
trotting through the centre of town

*

around midnight a drunk sings
the timing all wrong or right
modal song obscure innocent
walking medieval sleep

*

at two in the morning
a woman screaming
lying in the road,
a man without a shirt
- I'm sorry Esther, I'm sorry
three police cars
lights bouncing off the houses
lifting her up

another night, at the same door
Hey Joe
          Hey Joe

*

using order
using calm
mastering the heart

*

24

I bet you can tell me where I'm from.
Can I talk to you a minute? I've got
no one to talk to, you have. Have
you been shopping darling? I can see.
Look at this medal, my mother gave me
this. Look. I never knew her.

In the dream I was driving down a narrow lane to an English village where I was born, or through a dangerous and disputed border country.

The lane narrowed with overhanging trees and the hedgerows pressed in. I was lost and stuck with now way of returning. She beckoned me the way through. The colossus of earlier poems, dead now for nine years. All proportion is thrown.

She kindly takes the car and drives me through the tunnel of trees, the car is hers now. Her worn hand rests on me and I shrink. She reaches through the windscreen, which dissolves, and removes obstacles from our path.

She stands looking at me as I leave the car, I'm in exactly the right place to set out across the open hills. Then I know love is not a metaphor. Her love
surrounds me. It has only one name as I leave, turning to tell you when you wake.

One star rose this morning
weather walked over the slates,
from here you see every day
the air drawn circuit of birds,
light falls from the hills
moored at the back of the set.

Spring rushes into summer
floating dense green at the windows,
flooding along the road
- one way the park, the other town,
Odeon in red at the centre.

I walk towards the eastern gates,
the early traffic, dark transparent artifice
thinking to find the poem,
thinking to find the big way forward;
I began to write the book of all that happened,
I wake now writing the book of all that happened.

Cruising away from England at 33,000 feet
we saw you and waved but you didn't look up,
playing in a bright green square
your faces rise fresh in my mind

In the dream of falling I wanted to jump,
rush into the circuit of states and sculptured coasts
the real map of the air of desire,
dense like the language we spoke

Saying yes you would, so we jumped
bouncing off the wing into the blue harbour,
watching ourselves fall onto Cyprus
into the poppies of the necropolis outside Paphos

Oh set your arms around me,
hold on and let the wave lift us to the shore.

A white ship scratched
on a black pillar,
the sea retreated
out of memory the sea
sky salt marsh sky,
slow abstract disc
rising above us.

Then separate islands,
the black ship sighted.

The Aegean, a metaphor
(thinking it's) blue (literal)
not a metaphor,
the sun's path
over dot and dash waves,
the polished, sliding depth
crowded with dark messages.

By the harbour an off-shore island,
out of the air above the waves
Theseus abandoned Ariadne,
previously geometric, previously unknown,
you take a step down into the sanctuary.

Eating the fig in the shade of the well
we were drunk with seeing.
One time you could smell what the boats brought in
slice a tomato and smell it
like that, on the other side of the street.

Beyond the causeway, out of the sun,
the swimmer can see the submerged town;
collapsed doorways, shining paths,
step through marbled light, on the blue threshold
into deeper pressure I heard: Hello boy.

The sea rolled over our heads,
the thought of the next island or another person
ended here; the body of water crashing about us
delivered one word - love
and a terrible fight it was too.

On tracks through the dark hills
the sea wave bands all around us
the blue domed, white chapels,
and the unimagined cubist town
rises up as night lifts us into the sky.

Young marble giants sleep inside us,
that virtue which fills the body with itself,
limbs and head emerging from stone
if only I could, as if to take a step.
O you islands of men and women.

The free state does not come well arranged,
falling through the air of transmission
at every station we talk it over,
you've come to this place and it's inhabited,
at this hour all the radios play.
Terraces rise to the summit,
grit and the smell of thyme blown in your face.
The ten street lights of Kastro Hora
shine in a constellation under the stars,
Ouranos shines down in darkness to the sea.

at night the dark presence of
the trees by the side of the road
over us the whole country
turning into winter

Melanie you know where we are
it's the way back home
past where the children live
this is the literal poem of

night the dark trees
just here my sleeping girls
and where we go
rain shining the road

let's use the small map
its anthropomorphic spaces
coloured for the ordinary day
to save our lives

Respect

I would trace the air blue print
by the window in the high, white room
collect the days on this narrow table,
a bright promontory above the town
launched like a metaphor into nothing.

Traffic bears us back into lyric
into this explicit, personal experience
I would restore the working model,
we see the shops stacked and go to work
the shabby families rise and fall.

My family's reduced in the cold ground,
the old man bowed his head to listen; oh let go, let go.
She's selling the book of my country's impoverishment,
in all those channels meaning money.
You must outlive the misery of it.

I hope you're keeping some kind of record.
- I'm going random in Lavater in fact,
a strange land before the songs
in the fields of archaic sculpture
the pure body entirely present.

You must remember and forget everything,
tracts of the homeland reassigned
memory taken from us into other hands;
the republic all gone, all?
Don't fuss over terms, get into positions.

The nation's there only at night,
dark map cast on the air
station by station, the names restored
lighting the shape of another country,
the pure body entirely present.

Zion, a way of behaving, remember,
and those earthly stars, the next town
inagined as elements in the statement,
every item underfoot in the early hours
the ghost furniture and all that's happened.

When you wake and open your eyes
transparent days rise to the surface,
each part aligned on the grid
etched on the smooth face of the unworked block,
today's already horizontal light.

Shares fall in the Asian morning,
fear falls to earth and burns us;
numberless they clamour at the glass
cathedral clouds roll in from the west,
the sky opens to drench us to the skin.

Will you wake and open your eyes
or are you away in the big truth,
sailing the white ship to those islands.
Pull the sheet off your face boy,
it's a brand new day.

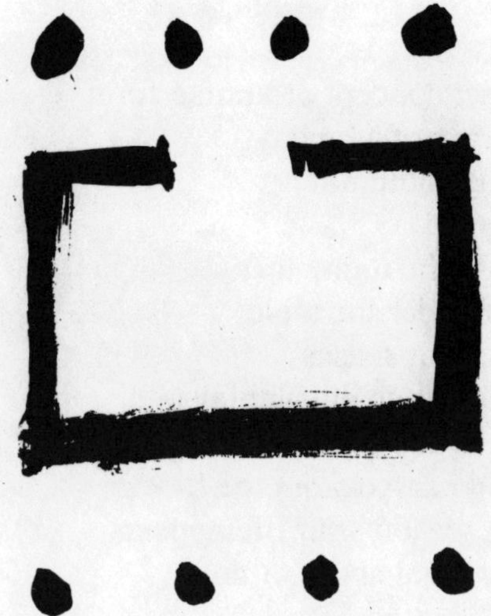

Athens

I saw an abstract concept of human form
outside in the rain of Monday
turning cold with autumn.

I saw you across the room
your good legs under the table,
the sky opening our senses
everyday this absolute music plays.

In the blue field carved from the block
without loss of reason your life appears,
you can get personal about or not.

Hands reach out and lights map
dark streets and familiar traffic,
in this unimagined town I imagine
I see your eyes, your face, your colour.

Athlone

This afternoon a summer wind
revealed the underside of leaves,
fields in waves all the way home
made green light to swim through.

I was the boy again, it was my picture,
look at these colours,
it was summer rolling out
and the personal dead lying down.

There are things not said in poetry:
the personal dead and the lying down light,
this casual breeze all over England
and the boy I was afraid to meet gone.

Nothing is lost in all that time,
it's my daughter saying - look my picture.

Hilversum

Saxon mouth, telling us how to live,
over the scabby allotments back there
but for the warmth in the name
even my sister, what do you expect?

It leaps up from the long table into your face:
at 1.20 dread wind slips into town,
at 1.20 total loss holds me.
There's no stepping back from here.

Standing outside the house
I thought we were dark bodies
walking through the light of facing windows;
another family lives there now.

It means don't believe that broadcast,
the time of your life or.

Home Service

Driving away from there
ground fog ankle deep in meadows
live radio cast before us,
the car packed with trophies.

Westward into big sky
deep in the dark fold,
ghosts drift over the fields
each boundary lined with snow.

Night silence gone down the tunnel
our view is immediate landscape,
the wealth of supermarkets
exploding for sheer enterprise.

The external narration is nothing.
Stop. Unload. I know where this can go.

Melanie's Book has been printed
in an edition of 300 copies
of which 26 are lettered A-Z
and signed by the author